Questions About Angels

PITT POETRY SERIES

Ed Ochester, Editor

Questions About Angels

POEMS

Billy Collins

University of Pittsburgh Press

Published 1999 by the University of Pittsburgh Press, Pittsburgh, Pa. 15261
Originally published by William Morrow and Company, Inc.
Copyright © 1991, Billy Collins
Manufactured in the United States of America
Printed on acid-free paper
10 9 8 7 6 5 4 .

Library of Congress Cataloging-in-Publication Data

Collins, Billy.
    Questions about angels : poems / Billy Collins.
        p.   cm. — (Pitt poetry series)
    ISBN 0-8229-5698-5 (alk. paper)
    I. Title. II. Series.
PS3553.047478Q47 1999
811'.54—dc21   98-45376

for Diane

CONTENTS

American Sonnet

We do not speak like Petrarch or wear a hat like Spenser
and it is not fourteen lines
like furrows in a small, carefully plowed field

but the picture postcard, a poem on vacation,
that forces us to sing our songs in little rooms
or pour our sentiments into measuring cups.

We write on the back of a waterfall or lake,
adding to the view a caption as conventional
as an Elizabethan woman's heliocentric eyes.

We locate an adjective for the weather.
We announce that we are having a wonderful time.
We express the wish that you were here

and hide the wish that we were where you are,
walking back from the mailbox, your head lowered
as you read and turn the thin message in your hands.

A slice of this place, a length of white beach,
a piazza or carved spires of a cathedral
will pierce the familiar place where you remain,

and you will toss on the table this reversible display:
a few square inches of where we have strayed
and a compression of what we feel.

A History of Weather

It is the kind of spring morning—candid sunlight
elucidating the air, a flower-ruffling breeze—
that makes me want to begin a history of weather,
a ten-volume elegy for the atmospheres of the past,
the envelopes that have moved around the moving globe.

It will open by examining the cirrus clouds
that are now sweeping over this house into the next state,
and every chapter will step backwards in time
to illustrate the rain that fell on battlefields
and the winds that attended beheadings, coronations.

The snow flurries of Victorian London will be surveyed
along with the gales that blew off Renaissance caps.
The tornadoes of the Middle Ages will be explicated
and the long, overcast days of the Dark Ages.
There will be a section on the frozen nights of antiquity
and on the heat that shimmered in the deserts of the Bible.

The study will be hailed as ambitious and definitive,
for it will cover even the climate before the Flood
when showers moistened Eden and will conclude
with the mysteries of the weather before history
when unseen clouds drifted over an unpeopled world,

when not a soul lay in any of earth's meadows gazing up
at the passing of enormous faces and animal shapes,
his jacket bunched into a pillow, an open book on his chest.

First Reader

I can see them standing politely on the wide pages
that I was still learning to turn,
Jane in a blue jumper, Dick with his crayon-brown hair,
playing with a ball or exploring the cosmos
of the backyard, unaware they are the first characters,
the boy and girl who begin fiction.

Beyond the simple illustration of their neighborhood
the other protagonists were waiting in a huddle:
frightening Heathcliff, frightened Pip, Nick Adams
carrying a fishing rod. Emma Bovary riding into Rouen.

But I would read about the perfect boy and his sister
even before I would read about Adam and Eve, garden and
     gate,
and before I heard the name Gutenberg, the type
of their simple talk was moving into my focusing eyes.

It was always Saturday and he and she
were always pointing at something and shouting "Look!"
pointing at the dog, the bicycle, or at their father
as he pushed a hand mower over the lawn,
waving at aproned mother framed in the kitchen doorway,
pointing toward the sky, pointing at each other.

They wanted us to look but we had looked already
and seen the shaded lawn, the wagon, the postman.
We had seen the dog, walked, watered and fed the animal,
and now it was time to discover the infinite, clicking
permutations of the alphabet's small and capital letters.
Alphabetical ourselves in the rows of classroom desks,
we were forgetting how to look, learning how to read.

Student of Clouds

The emotion is to be found in the clouds,
not in the green solids of the sloping hills
or even in the gray signatures of rivers,
according to Constable, who was a student of clouds
and filled shelves of sketchbooks with their motion,
their lofty gesturing and sudden implication of weather.

Outdoors, he must have looked up thousands of times,
his pencil trying to keep pace with their high voyaging
and the silent commotion of their eddying and flow.
Clouds would move beyond the outlines he would draw
as they moved within themselves, tumbling into their
    centers
and swirling off at the burning edges in vapors
to dissipate into the universal blue of the sky.

In photographs we can stop all this movement now
long enough to tag them with their Latin names.
Cirrus, nimbus, stratocumulus—
dizzying, romantic, authoritarian—
they bear their titles over the schoolhouses below
where their shapes and meanings are memorized.

High on the soft blue canvases of Constable
they are stuck in pigment but his clouds appear
to be moving still in the wind of his brush,
inching out of England and the nineteenth century
and sailing over these meadows where I am walking,
bareheaded beneath this cupola of motion,
my thoughts arranged like paint on a high blue ceiling.

Candle Hat

In most self-portraits it is the face that dominates:
Cézanne is a pair of eyes swimming in brushstrokes,
Van Gogh stares out of a halo of swirling darkness,
Rembrandt looks relieved as if he were taking a breather
from painting *The Blinding of Samson*.

But in this one Goya stands well back from the mirror
and is seen posed in the clutter of his studio
addressing a canvas tilted back on a tall easel.

He appears to be smiling out at us as if he knew
we would be amused by the extraordinary hat on his head
which is fitted around the brim with candle holders,
a device that allowed him to work into the night.

You can only wonder what it would be like
to be wearing such a chandelier on your head
as if you were a walking dining room or concert hall.

But once you see this hat there is no need to read
any biography of Goya or to memorize his dates.

To understand Goya you only have to imagine him
lighting the candles one by one, then placing
the hat on his head, ready for a night of work.

Imagine him surprising his wife with his new invention,
then laughing like a birthday cake when she saw the glow.

Imagine him flickering through the rooms of his house
with all the shadows flying across the walls.

Imagine a lost traveler knocking on his door
one dark night in the hill country of Spain.
"Come in," he would say, "I was just painting myself,"
as he stood in the doorway holding up the wand of a brush,
illuminated in the blaze of his famous candle hat.

The Death of Allegory

I am wondering what became of all those tall abstractions
that used to pose, robed and statuesque, in paintings
and parade about on the pages of the Renaissance
displaying their capital letters like license plates.

Truth cantering on a powerful horse,
Chastity, eyes downcast, fluttering with veils.
Each one was marble come to life, a thought in a coat,
Courtesy bowing with one hand always extended,

Villainy sharpening an instrument behind a wall,
Reason with her crown and Constancy alert behind a helm.
They are all retired now, consigned to a Florida for tropes.
Justice is there standing by an open refrigerator.

Valor lies in bed listening to the rain.
Even Death has nothing to do but mend his cloak and
    hood,
and all their props are locked away in a warehouse,
hourglasses, globes, blindfolds and shackles.

Even if you called them back, there are no places left
for them to go, no Garden of Mirth or Bower of Bliss.
The Valley of Forgiveness is lined with condominiums
and chain saws are howling in the Forest of Despair.

Here on the table near the window is a vase of peonies
and next to it black binoculars and a money clip,
exactly the kind of thing we now prefer,
objects that sit quietly on a line in lower case,

themselves and nothing more, a wheelbarrow,
an empty mailbox, a razor blade resting in a glass ashtray.
As for the others, the great ideas on horseback
and the long-haired virtues in embroidered gowns,

it looks as though they have traveled down
that road you see on the final page of storybooks,
the one that winds up a green hillside and disappears
into an unseen valley where everyone must be fast asleep.

Reading Myself to Sleep

The house is all in darkness except for this corner bedroom
where the lighthouse of a table lamp is guiding
my eyes through the narrow channels of print,

and the only movement in the night is the slight
swirl of curtains, the easy lift and fall of my breathing,
and the flap of pages as they turn in the wind of my hand.

Is there a more gentle way to go into the night
than to follow an endless rope of sentences
and then to slip drowsily under the surface of a page

into the first tentative flicker of a dream,
passing out of the bright precincts of attention
like cigarette smoke passing through a window screen?

All late readers know this sinking feeling of falling
into the liquid of sleep and then rising again
to the call of a voice that you are holding in your hands,

as if pulled from the sea back into a boat
where a discussion is raging on some subject or other,
on Patagonia or Thoroughbreds or the nature of war.

Is there a better method of departure by night
than this quiet bon voyage with an open book,
the sole companion who has come to see you off,

to wave you into the dark waters beyond language?
I can hear the rush and sweep of fallen leaves outside
where the world lies unconscious, and I can feel myself

dissolving, drifting into a story that will never be written,
letting the book slip to the floor where I will find it
in the morning when I surface, wet and streaked with
   daylight.

The Norton Anthology of
English Literature

It is easy to find out if a poet is a contemporary poet
and thus avoid the imbroglio of calling him Victorian
or worse, Elizabethan, or worse yet, medieval.

If you look him up in *The Norton Anthology of English
Literature*
and the year of his birth is followed only by a dash
and a small space for the numerals only spirits know,
then it is safe to say that he is probably alive,

perhaps out walking in a pale coat, inhaling the night air,
alive and contemporary as he lights a cigarette
and the smoke billows forth like an amorphous thought
dissipating over the cold, barge-heavy river he is staring
into.

But if the dash in the book is followed by another year,
he is not contemporary; perhaps he is nothing at all
save what remains on the few pages there for you to read
and maybe read over again, read aloud to an empty room.

Did you know that it is possible if you read a poem
enough times, if you read it over and over without
stopping,
that you can make the author begin to spin gently,
even affectionately, in his grave?

History is busy tonight in the freezing cemetery
carving death dates in stone with a hammer and chisel
and closing those parentheses that are used to embrace our
   lives,
as if we were afterthoughts dropped into a long sentence.

In the light of all this, I am thankful that I can even see
History standing there holding her allegorical tools.
And I am amazed at how tall and solemn she looks
and how immaculate are her robes.

The Hunt

Somewhere in the rolling hills and farm country
that lie beyond speech
Noah Webster and his assistants are moving
across the landscape tracking down a new word.

It is a small noun about the size of a mouse,
one that will be seldom used by anyone,
like a synonym for *isthmus,*
but they are pursuing the creature zealously

as if it were the verb *to be,*
swinging their sticks and calling out to one another
as they wade through a field of waist-high barley.

Forgetfulness

The name of the author is the first to go
followed obediently by the title, the plot,
the heartbreaking conclusion, the entire novel
which suddenly becomes one you have never read, never
  even heard of,

as if, one by one, the memories you used to harbor
decided to retire to the southern hemisphere of the brain,
to a little fishing village where there are no phones.

Long ago you kissed the names of the nine Muses goodbye
and watched the quadratic equation pack its bag,
and even now as you memorize the order of the planets,

something else is slipping away, a state flower perhaps,
the address of an uncle, the capital of Paraguay.

Whatever it is you are struggling to remember
it is not poised on the tip of your tongue,
not even lurking in some obscure corner of your spleen.

It has floated away down a dark mythological river
whose name begins with an *L* as far as you can recall,

well on your own way to oblivion where you will join those
who have even forgotten how to swim and how to ride a
  bicycle.

No wonder you rise in the middle of the night
to look up the date of a famous battle in a book on war.
No wonder the moon in the window seems to have drifted
out of a love poem that you used to know by heart.

2

Questions About Angels

Of all the questions you might want to ask
about angels, the only one you ever hear
is how many can dance on the head of a pin.

No curiosity about how they pass the eternal time
besides circling the Throne chanting in Latin
or delivering a crust of bread to a hermit on earth
or guiding a boy and girl across a rickety wooden bridge.

Do they fly through God's body and come out singing?
Do they swing like children from the hinges
of the spirit world saying their names backwards and
    forwards?
Do they sit alone in little gardens changing colors?

What about their sleeping habits, the fabric of their robes,
their diet of unfiltered divine light?
What goes on inside their luminous heads? Is there a wall
these tall presences can look over and see hell?

If an angel fell off a cloud would he leave a hole
in a river and would the hole float along endlessly
filled with the silent letters of every angelic word?

If an angel delivered the mail would he arrive
in a blinding rush of wings or would he just assume
the appearance of the regular mailman and
whistle up the driveway reading the postcards?

No, the medieval theologians control the court.
The only question you ever hear is about
the little dance floor on the head of a pin
where halos are meant to converge and drift invisibly.

It is designed to make us think in millions,
billions, to make us run out of numbers and collapse
into infinity, but perhaps the answer is simply one:
one female angel dancing alone in her stocking feet,
a small jazz combo working in the background.

She sways like a branch in the wind, her beautiful
eyes closed, and the tall thin bassist leans over
to glance at his watch because she has been dancing
forever, and now it is very late, even for musicians.

A Wonder of the World

It is just now coming into view.
You can begin to make out its westerly corner
and you are now getting some idea of its dimensions.

As we continue to maintain this heading
more of it will gradually be revealed,
the mountain appearing to step aside to permit a fuller
   view.

At this point you can see a great deal of it.
It is more colossal than you had expected,
and you were not at all prepared for its look

of almost archaeological seriousness
as if you should be wearing steel-rimmed spectacles
in order to view it properly.

Now you are able to see the whole thing, in moonlight!
Nothing is standing between you and it
except an immeasurable volume of salty night air.

It looks different than it does in photographs
and it is nothing like what you had imagined,
but there it is, motionless, unavoidable, real.

It is enough to make you reach for the locket
in which you carry your picture of the world
as you glide closer and closer to it
over the cold streaming surface of these waters.

Mappamundi

On the pages I am turning are early pictures of the world,
the continents and oceans so erroneously shaped
it is hard to tell which is which at first,
as if they were drawn by a child or someone blindfolded.

Along the shorelines, tiny ships are under sail,
blown by the pursed mouth of a cloud with an angry face,
and sea beasts prowl the waves that lap at the margins
where knowledge trails off and ink lines squiggle
into a vast unknown, an incognita

far from the old garden of Europe in the center
where the mapmaker sits bent over his slanted desk,
touching the contours of the earth with the tip of his pen.

The library windows are streaming with summer rain
as I sit bent over this book of ancient maps,
feeling how the edges of my own world blur into tundra
and imagining what monsters must be illustrated there
far from the middle of what little I know.

But I am oriented here, encased in a local thunderstorm,
flipping through these imagined worlds, noticing
that east, not north, is always at the top where mornings

begin and discovering at the bottom of one intricate page
an early version of Australia, so far from anything
that it even has its own sun drawn in the sky overhead.

Now that is the kind of sun I would like to be under
this afternoon, basking naked on an arc of beach
at the end of the world while sea monsters writhe offshore,

then lying down prone on the sand, my arms stretched out
so wide I can feel the slight curvature of the earth
as I work effortlessly on my imaginary tan.

The First Geniuses

It is so early almost nothing has happened.
Agriculture is an unplanted seed.
Music and the felt hat are thousands of years away.
The sail and the astrolabe, not even specks on the horizon.
The window and scissors: inconceivable.

But even now, before the orchestra of history
has had time to warm up, the first geniuses
have found one another and gathered into a thoughtful
    group.
Gaunt, tall and bearded, as you might expect,
they stand outlined against a landscape of smoking
    volcanoes

or move along the shores of lakes, still leaden and unnamed,
or sit on high bare cliffs looking like early arrivals
at a party the earth is about to throw
now that the dinosaurs have finally cleared the room.

They have yet to discover fire, much less invent the wheel,
so they wander a world mostly dark and motionless
wondering what to do with their wisdom
like young girls wonder what to do with their hair.

Once in a while someone will make a pronouncement
about the movement of the stars, the density of silence,
or the strange behavior of water in winter,
but there is no alphabet, not a drop of ink on earth,
so the words disappear into the deep green forests
like flocks of small, startled birds.

Eventually one of them will come up with the compass
or draw the first number in sand with a stick,
and he will let out a shout like Archimedes in his tub
and curious animals will look up from their grazing.

Later the water screw and the catapult will appear;
the nail, the speedometer and the bow tie will follow.
But until then they can only pace the world gravely,
knowing nothing but the thrumming of their minds,
not the whereabouts of north or the notion of zero,
not even how to sharpen a stone to a deadly point.

The Afterlife

While you are preparing for sleep, brushing your teeth,
or riffling through a magazine in bed,
the dead of the day are setting out on their journey.

They are moving off in all imaginable directions,
each according to his own private belief,
and this is the secret that silent Lazarus would not reveal:
that everyone is right, as it turns out.
You go to the place you always thought you would go,
the place you kept lit in an alcove in your head.

Some are being shot up a funnel of flashing colors
into a zone of light, white as a January sun.
Others are standing naked before a forbidding judge who
    sits
with a golden ladder on one side, a coal chute on the other.

Some have already joined the celestial choir
and are singing as if they have been doing this forever,
while the less inventive find themselves stuck
in a big air-conditioned room full of food and chorus girls.

Some are approaching the apartment of the female God,
a woman in her forties with short wiry hair
and glasses hanging from her neck by a string.
With one eye she regards the dead through a hole in her
   door.

There are those who are squeezing into the bodies
of animals—eagles and leopards—and one trying on
the skin of a monkey like a tight suit,
ready to begin another life in a more simple key,

while others float off into some benign vagueness,
little units of energy heading for the ultimate elsewhere.

There are even a few classicists being led to an underworld
by a mythological creature with a beard and hooves.
He will bring them to the mouth of a furious cave
guarded over by Edith Hamilton and her three-headed dog.

The rest just lie on their backs in their coffins
wishing they could return so they could learn Italian
or see the pyramids, or play some golf in a light rain.
They wish they could wake in the morning like you
and stand at a window examining the winter trees,
every branch traced with the ghost writing of snow.

The Dead

The dead are always looking down on us, they say,
while we are putting on our shoes or making a sandwich,
they are looking down through the glass-bottom boats of
  heaven
as they row themselves slowly through eternity.

They watch the tops of our heads moving below on earth,
and when we lie down in a field or on a couch,
drugged perhaps by the hum of a warm afternoon,
they think we are looking back at them,

which makes them lift their oars and fall silent
and wait, like parents, for us to close our eyes.

Endangered

It is so quiet on the shore of this motionless lake
you can hear the slow recessional of extinct animals
as they leave through a door at the back of the world,
disappearing like the verbs of a dead language:

the last troop of kangaroos hopping out of the picture,
the ultimate paddling of ducks and pitying of turtledoves
and, his bell tolling in the distance, the final goat.

Going Out for Cigarettes

It's a story as famous as the three little pigs:
one evening a man says he is going out for cigarettes,
closes the door behind him and is never heard from again,
not one phone call, not even a postcard from Rio.

For all anyone knows, he walks straight into the distance
like a line from Euclid's notebooks and vanishes
with the smoke he blows into the soft humid air,
smoke that forms a screen, smoke to calm the bees within.

He has his fresh pack, an overcoat with big pockets.
What else does he need as he walks beyond city limits,
past the hedges, porch lights and empty cars of the suburbs
and into a realm no larger than his own hat size?

Alone, he is a solo for piano that never comes to an end,
a small plane that keeps flying away from the earth.
He is the last line of a poem that continues off the page
and down to a river to drag there in the cool flow,

questioning the still pools with its silver hook.
Let us say this is the place where the man who goes out
for cigarettes finally comes to rest: on a riverbank
above the long, inquisitive wriggling of that line,

sitting content in the quiet picnic of consciousness,
nothing on his mind as he lights up another one,
nothing but the arc of the stone bridge he notices
downstream, and its upturned reflection in the water.

3

Purity

My favorite time to write is in the late afternoon,
weekdays, particularly Wednesdays.
This is how I go about it:
I take a fresh pot of tea into my study and close the door.
Then I remove my clothes and leave them in a pile
as if I had melted to death and my legacy consisted of only
a white shirt, a pair of pants and a pot of cold tea.

Then I remove my flesh and hang it over a chair.
I slide it off my bones like a silken garment.
I do this so that what I write will be pure,
completely rinsed of the carnal,
uncontaminated by the preoccupations of the body.

Finally I remove each of my organs and arrange them
on a small table near the window.
I do not want to hear their ancient rhythms
when I am trying to tap out my own drumbeat.

Now I sit down at the desk, ready to begin.
I am entirely pure: nothing but a skeleton at a typewriter.

I should mention that sometimes I leave my penis on.
I find it difficult to ignore the temptation.
Then I am a skeleton with a penis at a typewriter.

In this condition I write extraordinary love poems,
most of them exploiting the connection between sex and
    death.

I am concentration itself: I exist in a universe
where there is nothing but sex, death, and typewriting.

After a spell of this I remove my penis too.
Then I am all skull and bones typing into the afternoon.
Just the absolute essentials, no flounces.
Now I write only about death, most classical of themes
in language light as the air between my ribs.

Afterward, I reward myself by going for a drive at sunset.
I replace my organs and slip back into my flesh
and clothes. Then I back the car out of the garage
and speed through woods on winding country roads,
passing stone walls, farmhouses, and frozen ponds,
all perfectly arranged like words in a famous sonnet.

Cliché

My life is an open book. It lies here
on a glass tabletop, its pages shamelessly exposed,
outspread like a bird with hundreds of thin paper wings.

It is a biography, needless to say,
and I am reading and writing it simultaneously
in a language troublesome and private.
Every reader must be a translator with a thick lexicon.

No one has read the whole thing but me.
Most dip into the middle for a few paragraphs,
then move on to other shelves, other libraries.
Some have time only for the illustrations.

I love to feel the daily turning of the pages,
the sentences unwinding like string,
and when something really important happens,
I walk out to the edge of the page
and, always the student,
make an asterisk, a little star, in the margin.

Field Guide

No one I ask knows the name of the flower
we pulled the car to the side of the road to pick
and that I point to dangling purple from my lapel.

I am passing through the needle of spring
in North Carolina, as ignorant of the flowers of the south
as the woman at the barbecue stand who laughs
and the man who gives me a look as he pumps the gas

and everyone else I ask on the way to the airport
to return to where this purple madness is not seen
blazing against the sober pines and rioting along the
    roadside.

On the plane, the stewardess is afraid she cannot answer
my question, now insistent with the fear that I will leave
the province of this flower without its sound in my ear.

Then, as if he were giving me the time of day, a passenger
looks up from his magazine and says *wisteria*.

Putti in the Night

It is raining so hard and the jazz on the radio
is playing so loud, you almost feel like surrendering
to the wish that somebody up there actually liked you
or at least was keeping an eye on your solitude.
Not necessarily God himself, glaring down through the roof
while he fingers a weighty book looking for your name.

You would rather be canopied by a small group of putti,
those angels in their infancy always hovering
in the upper, vaporous corners of religious paintings.

Chubby little witnesses treading the light blue air,
they look as if they had just tumbled out of paradise,
noticed the Ascension or the Birth of the Virgin
going on below and fluttered over to take a look.

You have seen them too in sumptuous portrayals of love,
dropping rose petals, letting arrows fly from tiny bows
above a scene of immense silks, bosoms and men with
    swords.
Imagine leaning back in your chair and beholding
an aggregation of those weightless, buoyant babies above,
trailing their clouds of glory, casting smiles upon your life.

But it is doubtful that they will be attending you tonight,
though the hour is late and the music has become so slow
you have to wait for every half note to fall into place
like pieces dropping from heaven into a puzzle.

Even if you were a saint, how could you travel back
to the Renaissance and find someone to paint you
with the putti floating over your halo, your sandals,
your coarse brown robe and wild, uplifted eyes?
And would you say that your loving deserves such sweet
levitation, such a feathery, ethereal regard?

Better to turn up the music loud enough to hear
outside, better to take a walk on the darkened lawn
and trade all this in for a new swarm of thoughts.
The rain is lighter now, atomized and soft upon your face.
It makes you stop and listen to Bud Powell pounding
in the silence and feel the old embrace of earth and sky.

The Man in the Moon

He used to frighten me in the nights of childhood,
the wide adult face, enormous, stern, aloft.
I could not imagine such loneliness, such coldness.

But tonight as I drive home over these hilly roads
I see him sinking behind stands of winter trees
and rising again to show his familiar face.

And when he comes into full view over open fields
he looks like a young man who has fallen in love
with the dark earth,

a pale bachelor, well-groomed and full of melancholy,
his round mouth open
as if he had just broken into song.

Horseman, Pass By!

When I show you the photograph of me
leaning on the tombstone of Yeats,
you are surprised that I never noticed
the photograph of *you* leaning on it,
in a metal frame above your desk.

So many caravans of tour buses stop
at Drumcliff's little churchyard these days
there must be enough color photographs
of people leaning against that limestone slab,
casting a cold eye at the camera,

to fill an archive rivaling the archives
of people leaning on the Eiffel Tower or a sphinx,
cartons of these glossy shards of travel
stacked along the walls as the night watchman
works his crossword under a lamp etc., etc.

But still, when forced to backtrack down
that road I remember feeling myself touch
the brake, lift the directional stick and pull
like gravity into the muddy carpark.
Little point in standing again by his grave
where the picture was taken just three days before,

so I stayed in the car, low music on the radio,
holding a map, and letting the distance increase
between me and that phantom self
who could just drive by and now was miles away.

Memento Mori

There is no need for me to keep a skull on my desk,
to stand with one foot up on the ruins of Rome,
or wear a locket with the sliver of a saint's bone.

It is enough to realize that every common object
in this sunny little room will outlive me—
the carpet, radio, bookstand and rocker.

Not one of these things will attend my burial,
not even this dented goosenecked lamp
with its steady benediction of light,

though I could put worse things in my mind
than the image of it waddling across the cemetery
like an old servant, dragging the tail of its cord,
the small circle of mourners parting to make room.

The Last Man on Earth

Once there was a time when the moon swept
over the hemlocks, lawns and white mountaintops
of the earth, but now it only hides its face against my
   chest.

It used to pull sleepers from the lagoons of dreams
where they floated facedown,
but now it only lures me to an open window, curtains
billowing around my head like useless, delicate sails.

Weather used to ride high over the world
like an announcement nailed to the sky,
but now the cold wind has become my favorite song,
and I sing along in the only house with lights.

Clouds that once toured the air in the style
of dirigibles now gather helplessly in the kitchen
and stare at me across the long wooden table.

This morning when I put on my shoes they seemed
important, like the north and south poles,
and when I walked out and heard the noise of geese
I looked up as if they were calling my name.

Come Running

I spot the neighbor's dog scampering across the lawn
with my name in its mouth,
leaving me to wander through the house anonymously
and scour the telephone directory for an alias.

When I say my name out loud it sounds like
someone else's, a character in a play who cheats
the hero and comes to a bad end, or an obscure
athlete lost in the deep encyclopedia of baseball.

When I try writing it down on paper
I find I have also lost my signature. My hand
feels retarded, unable to perform its inky trick,
that unmistakable, eerie, Arabic flourish.

Perhaps the dog was never given a name
and is now eating mine with pleasure
under a porch in the cool, lattice-shadowed dirt.

Perhaps late tonight I will hear the voice
of my neighbor as she stands at her back door,
hands cupped around her mouth, calling my name,
and I will leap the hedge and come running.

Modern Peasant

This morning is the same as all other mornings.
I part the window curtain and the familiar play begins.
Sunlight keeps repeating itself as if I were blind.
The same black car waits in the driveway for my key,
my manipulations and the sound of its radio.

It is the same old song, blue exit signs enlarging
and disappearing behind the stream of my travel
as I think about the past, that rope I drag along,
and the future which is the rope that pulls me forward.

Ah, but tonight I will drink red wine at dinner.
I will continue to drink red wine after dinner.
Then I will lie down in the dark greens of the lawn
and think of something entirely new.

I will feel the rotation of the earth
as electrically as the sudden touch of a stranger.
I will wonder how many thousands of days
it would take the two of us to walk to the moon.

Instructions to the Artist

I wish my head to appear perfectly round
and since the canvas should be of epic dimensions,
please trace the circle with a dinner plate
rather than a button or a dime.

My face should be painted with
an ant-like sense of detail;
pretend you are executing a street map
of Rome and that all the citizens
can lift thirty times their own weight.

The result should be a strained
but self-satisfied expression,
as if I am lifting a Volkswagen with one foot.

The body is no great matter;
just draw some straight lines
with a pencil and ruler.
I will not be around to hear the voice
of posterity calling me Stickman.

The background I leave up to you
but if there is to be a house,
lines of smoke rising from the chimney

should be mandatory.
Never be ashamed of kindergarten—
it is the alphabet's only temple.

Also, have several kangaroos grazing
and hopping around in the distance,
an allusion to my world travels.

Some final recommendations:
I should like to appear hatless.
Kindly limit your palette to a single
primary color, any one but red or blue.
Sign the painting on my upper lip
so your name will always be my mustache.

Weighing the Dog

It is awkward for me and bewildering for him
as I hold him in my arms in the small bathroom,
balancing our weight on the shaky blue scale,

but this is the way to weigh a dog and easier
than training him to sit obediently on one spot
with his tongue out, waiting for the cookie.

With pencil and paper I subtract my weight
from our total to find out the remainder that is his,
and I start to wonder if there is an analogy here.

It could not have to do with my leaving you
though I never figured out what you amounted to
until I subtracted myself from our combination.

You held me in your arms more than I held you
through all those awkward and bewildering months
and now we are both lost in strange and distant
    neighborhoods.

One Life to Live

This is the only life I have, this one in my head,
the one that travels along the surface of my body
singing the low voltage song of the ego,

the one that feels like a ball between my ears
sometimes, and other times feels absolutely galactic,

the life that my feet carry around like two blind
scholars working together on a troublesome manuscript.

This is the only life I have, and I am standing
dead in the center of it like a man doing a rope trick
in a rodeo, passing the lasso over his body,
smiling inside a twirling of ovals and ellipses.

This is the only life I have and I never step out of it
except to follow a character down the alleys of a novel
or when love makes me want to remove my clothes
and sail classical records off a cliff.

Otherwise you can always find me within this hoop of
   myself,
the rope flying around me, moving up to encircle my head
like an equator or a halo or a zero.

The Wires of the Night

I thought about his death for so many hours,
tangled there in the wires of the night,
that it came to have a body and dimensions,
more than a voice shaking over the telephone
or the black obituary boldface of name and dates.

His death now had an entrance and an exit, doors and
    stairs,
windows and shutters which are the motionless wings
of windows. His death had a head and clothes,
the white shirt and baggy trousers of death.

His death had pages, a dark leather cover, an index,
and the print was too minuscule for anyone to read.
His death had hinges and bolts which were oiled and
    locked,
had a loud motor, four tires, an antenna which listened
to the wind, and a mirror in which you could see the past.

His death had sockets and keys, it had walls and beams.
It had a handle which you could not hold and a floor
you could not lie down on in the middle of the night.

In the freakish pink and grey of dawn I took
his death to bed with me and his death was my bed
and in every corner of the room it hid from the light,

and then it was the light of day and the next day
and all the days to follow, and it moved into the future
like the sharp tip of a pen moving across an empty page.

Axiom

"Life is beautiful. Life is sad."
— NABOKOV

And the two are braided together
like the long hair of a woman
who is about to die suddenly.

She arranges a vase of flowers,
takes a coat from the closet.
She regards herself in a mirror.

She is leaving the house,
closing the door behind her.
There is no stopping her.

The sadness is the bread
and the beauty is the wine
or the other way around.

I have been visited by a thought
contoured like an automobile:
beautiful.

Then again, I am lying under
all the clothes of the dead,
feeling every ton
as they add more to the pile.

Vade Mecum

I want the scissors to be sharp
and the table to be perfectly level
when you cut me out of my life
and paste me in that book you always carry.

Not Touching

The valentine of desire is pasted over my heart
and still we are not touching, like things

in a poorly done still life
where the knife appears to be floating over the plate
which is itself hovering above the table somehow,

the entire arrangement of apple, pear and wineglass
having forgotten the law of gravity,
refusing to be still,

as if the painter had caught them all
in a rare moment of slow flight
just before they drifted out of the room
through a window of perfectly realistic sunlight.

Night Sand

When you injure me, as you must one day,
I will move off like the slow armadillo over night sand,
ambulating secretly inside his armor,

ready to burrow deep or curl himself into a ball
which will shelter his soft head, soft feet
and tail from the heavy, rhythmic blows.

Now can you see the silhouettes of ranchers' hats
and sticks raised against the pink desert sky?

Love in the Sahara

The small camel leaves his common place
on the front of the pack of cigarettes
and sways across the floorboards in search of water.

His absence leaves a vacuum as eerie
as the one you left in our rented house,
empty as a desert without its furniture.

I never thought I would find myself smoking here
on this flat stretch of uncountable sand,
a forlorn illustration of figure and ground,

my only company the tiny pyramids and palms
planted in the distance, and the man
whose shirt pocket I ride in all afternoon.

Invective

Turn away from me, you, and get lost in the past.
Back to ancient Rome you go, with its parallel columns and
  syllogisms.
Stuff yourself with berries, eat lying on your side.
Suck balls of snow carried down from the Alps for dessert.

I don't care. I am leaving too, but for the margins of
  history,
to a western corner of ninth century Ireland I go,
to a vanishing, grey country far beyond your call.

There I will dwell with badgers, fish and deer,
birds piercing the air and the sound of little bells.
I will stand in pastures of watercress by the salmon-lashing
  sea.
I will stare into the cold, unblinking eyes of cows.

4

The Life of Riley: A Definitive Biography

He was born one sunny Florida morning
and napped through most of his childhood.
He spent his adult life relaxing in beach chairs,
always a tropical drink in his hand.

He never had a job, a family or a sore throat.
He never mowed a lawn.
Passersby would always stop to remind him
whose life it was he was living.
He died in a hammock weighing a cloud.

Jack

Just when I am about to telephone her
so she can hear me swallowing my pride,
a thing the size of a watermelon,

a giant barges out of a fairy tale,
picks up the house by the chimney
and carries it off laughing like thunder.
She will never believe this I tell myself.

From the windowsill where I hang on
I can see geysers of plumbing,
the exposed basement embarrassed by its junk,
snapped telephone wires on the lawn,
and the neighbors looking up with little
apocalypse expressions on their faces.

I realize on the way up the beanstalk
apologizing over the phone was a bad idea.
A letter provides a more reflective means
of saying hard things, expressing true feelings.

If there is pen and paper in his kingdom,
I plan to write her a long vivid one
communicating my ardor, but also describing

the castle floating in high clouds,
the goose, the talking musical instruments,
and the echo of his enormous shoes.

In fact, to convince her of my unwavering love,
I will compose it while pacing back and forth
in his palm.

Metamorphosis

If Kafka could turn a man into an insect in one sentence
perhaps he could transform me into something new,
a slow willful river running through a forest,
or simply the German word for river, a handful of letters
hidden in the dark alphabetical order of a dictionary.

Not that I am so miserable, but I could use a change
of scenery and substance, plus the weather reminds me of
    him.
I imagine Kafka at his desk: the nib of his pen,
like the beak of a bird, disturbs the surface of a pool of ink,
and he writes a sentence at the top of a page

changing me into a goldfish or a lost mitten
or a cord of split wood or the New York Public Library.
Ah, to awaken one morning as the New York Public
    Library.
I would pass the days observing old men in raincoats
as they mounted the ponderous steps between the lions

carrying wild and scribbled notes inside their pockets.
I would feel the pages of books turning inside me like
    butterflies.
I would stare over Fifth Avenue with a perfectly straight
    face.

Saturday Morning

I wonder if I have become smaller or has the bedroom
always been the size of a western state.
The aspirin bottle is in the medicine cabinet
two hundred miles away, a six day ride,
and my robe hangs from the closet door in another time
   zone.

A strange circumstance for one who was a giant king
last night in a principality of thimbles
where all money was smaller than dimes
and the flag over my castle displayed a flea.

But no matter. The television is right next to the bed
and Donald Duck is taking his nephews ice-skating.

Late Show

No wonder everyone loved the private dick
whose only badge is a pack of Camels
and who never dies until the movie is over
and nobody can watch him writhe.

He charges a hundred a day plus expenses,
and there would be plenty of time to relax
between cases.

The only suffering in the world would be
those blackjackings from the blind side,
his nods to mortality,

but then he fades into a soft dissolve
and comes to on a sumptuous couch,
a blonde in a nightgown rubbing his temples
and pouring brandies as she reconsiders
the doublecross.

What better style of transport
than an open car squealing along
the Coast Highway, one hand on the wheel
as you unravel the onion of the murder
so fast even she can't follow.

What better place to think things over
than a swivel chair in a darkened office,
the pulse of the neon hotel sign
illuminating your notorious face,

your hat hanging on the rack where you
tossed it on the way in.

Pie Man

I am carrying my homemade pies down a cobblestone road
that winds through a hamlet, balancing one pie
on each palm, traversing a page of fair watercolors
and ink lines, a white baker's hat collapsed on my head,
a white apron waving over my river blue pants.

Wives call to me from the frames of their cottage windows.
Children skip alongside me, their sunny faces uplifted.
My high jaunty strides show I love my trade.

You may remember the first time you saw me,
sitting in someone's lap as she turned the pages
of a thin book dropped long ago on the banks of childhood.

You may even remember some details like the rows
of fork holes in the crusts, the rising curlicues of steam,
my buckled shoes, the red lettering on my handcart.

It is a picture that will soon pale as it did before,
the pies, the hat, cobblestones and children breaking
into pieces and drifting off as objects do in space.

This may be the last time you think of me or I of you.
Think of the color of the shutters, the painted bridge,
the shapes of clouds, the wooden sign above the cheese
    shop.

Wolf

A wolf is reading a book of fairy tales.
The moon hangs over the forest, a lamp.

He is not assuming a human position,
say, cross-legged against a tree,
as he would in a cartoon.

This is a real wolf, standing on all fours,
his rich fur bristling in the night air,
his head bent over the book open on the ground.

He does not sit down for the words
would be too far away to be legible,
and it is with difficulty that he turns
each page with his nose and forepaws.

When he finishes the last tale
he lies down in pine needles.
He thinks about what he has read,
the stories passing over his mind
like the clouds crossing the moon.

A zigzag of wind shakes down hazelnuts.
The eyes of owls yellow in the branches.

The wolf now paces restlessly in circles
around the book until he is absorbed
by the power of its narration,
making him one of its illustrations,
a small paper wolf, flat as print.

Later that night, lost in a town of pigs,
he knocks over houses with his breath.

The History Teacher

Trying to protect his students' innocence
he told them the Ice Age was really just
the Chilly Age, a period of a million years
when everyone had to wear sweaters.

And the Stone Age became the Gravel Age,
named after the long driveways of the time.

The Spanish Inquisition was nothing more
than an outbreak of questions such as
"How far is it from here to Madrid?"
"What do you call the matador's hat?"

The War of the Roses took place in a garden,
and the Enola Gay dropped one tiny atom
on Japan.

The children would leave his classroom
for the playground to torment the weak
and the smart,
mussing up their hair and breaking their glasses,

while he gathered up his notes and walked home
past flower beds and white picket fences,
wondering if they would believe that soldiers
in the Boer War told long, rambling stories
designed to make the enemy nod off.

Pensée

All of Paris must have been away on holiday
when Pascal said that men are not happy
because they are incapable of staying in their rooms.

It is the kind of thought that belongs in a room,
sealed off from the vanities of the world,
polished roadsters, breasts, hunting lodges,
all letdowns in the end.

But imagine Columbus examining the wallpaper,
Magellan straightening up the dresser,
Lindbergh rearranging some magazines on a table.

Not to mention the need for everyday explorations,
the wandering we do, randomly as ants,
when we rove through woods without direction
or allow the diagram of a foreign city to lead us
through long afternoons of unpronounceable streets.

Then we are like children in playgrounds
who are discovering the art of running in circles
as if they were scribbling on the earth with their bodies.

We die only when we run out of footprints.
Then the biographers move in to retrace our paths,
enclosing them in tall mazes of lumber
to make our lives seem more complex, more arduous,
to make our leaving the room seem heroic.

The Discovery of Scat

Long before Dizzy,
high on the rising tower at Babel

a bearded carpenter turned
to a stonemason

(barely able to see him
through the veil of clouds),

turned to ask for a wooden nail
and said something
that sounded like
bop ah dooolyah bop.

Dog

I can hear him out in the kitchen,
his lapping the night's only music,
head bowed over the waterbowl
like an illustration in a book for boys.

He enters the room with such etiquette,
licking my bare ankle as if he understood
the Braille of the skin.

Then he makes three circles around himself,
flattening his ancient memory of tall grass
before dropping his weight with a sigh on the floor.

This is the spot where he will spend the night,
his ears listening for the syllable of his name,
his tongue hidden in his long mouth
like a strange naked hermit in a cave.

The Willies

"Public restrooms give me the willies."
— AD FOR A DISINFECTANT

There is no known cure for them,
unlike the heeby-jeebies
or the shakes

which Russian vodka and a hot bath
will smooth out.

The drifties can be licked,
though the vapors often spell trouble.

The whips-and-jangles
go away in time. So do the fantods.
And good company will put the blues
to flight

and do much to relieve the flips,
the quivers and the screamies.

But the willies are another matter.

Anything can give them to you:
electric chairs, raw meat, manta rays,
public restrooms, a footprint,
and every case of the willies
is a bad one.

Some say flow with them, ride them out,
but this is useless advice
once you are in their grip.

There is no way to get on top
of the willies. Valium
is ineffective. Hospitals
are not the answer.

Keeping still
and emitting thin, evenly spaced
waves of irony
may help

but don't expect miracles:
the willies are the willies.

On Reading in the Morning Paper That Dreams May Be Only Nonsense

We might have guessed as much, given the nightly
absurdities, the extravagant circus of the dark.
You hit the pillow and moments later your mother
appears as a llama, shouting at you in another language.

Or you find yourself drowning in a sea of breasts,
or drowning in a sea of basketballs—
those who have attended night school will be quick
to explain the difference.

Or the nonsense is just a scrambling of the day before,
everyone walking around the office stark naked,
the elevator doors opening on to deep space,
the clamshells from lunch floating by in slow motion.

Too bad Freud isn't here to hear this news,
maybe some pharaohs too, druids and wide-eyed diviners,
all gathered around my kitchen table
in their exotic clothes, their pale mouths moving
silently, as in a dream,

and me pouring coffee for everyone, proffering smokes,
pacing around in my bathrobe reading the paper out loud.

But the scene would soon swirl away
and I would find myself alone in some fix,
screaming within the confines of an hourglass,
being driven to the opera by a blind chauffeur

or waking up to the chilling evidence on the bedroom floor:
a small pile of sand, a white bow tie.

Rip Van Winkle

The illustrations always portray him outdoors,
sleeping at the base of a generous oak,
acorns bouncing off his elfin cap,
the beard grown over him like a blanket.

Here reclines the patron saint of sleep.
He has sawed enough logs to heat the Land of Nod.
His dreams are longer than all of Homer.
And the Z above his head looks anchored in the air.

You would think a forest animal would trouble
his slumber, the paw of a bear on his paunch,
but squirrels hop over his benign figure
and by now the birds are unafraid of his rhythmic snoring.

In the next valley the world probably goes on,
hammering and yelling and staying up late at night
while around his head flowers open and close
and leaves or snow fall as he sleeps through the seasons.

Some mornings, awakened by the opera of dawn,
I think of his recumbrance, his serene repose
as I open my eyes after a paltry eight hours,
pointlessly alert, gaudy with consciousness.

English Country House

I pass under the arched entrance to my hedge-maze
and move into its argument of corridors,
running a hand along the leafy walls, perfectly trimmed.
I love to move like a mouse inside this puzzle for the body,
balancing the wish to be lost with the need to be found.

I continue into the secret patterns of its side-lanes,
savoring the conundrum of every manicured corner and
　　turn.
At the end of a cul-de-sac I sit down on a white bench,
a place to rest and bask in one's befuddlement.

Then I walk on trying to forget the guests I abandoned.
I should be with them now wilting in a lawn chair
and talking over tea and lemon slices instead of watching
clouds pass over this crazy bower, this sweet labyrinth.

But people are not captivating as they were a decade ago
when the famous would come here to follow their
　　diversions,
Stubbs agitating over a sketchbook of Thoroughbreds,
Muybridge outdoors taking photographs of a naked boxer.

I remember Johann Mälzel inventing the metronome
in an upper room. In this soft afternoon light
I remember Roget walking up from the meadow,
his basket full of synonyms, the dogs barking at his clothes.
I remember them all as I stand here in the dark green
center.

Nostalgia

Remember the 1340s? We were doing a dance called the
   Catapult.
You always wore brown, the color craze of the decade,
and I was draped in one of those capes that were popular,
the ones with unicorns and pomegranates in needlework.
Everyone would pause for beer and onions in the afternoon,
and at night we would play a game called "Find the Cow."
Everything was hand-lettered then, not like today.

Where has the summer of 1572 gone? Brocade and sonnet
marathons were the rage. We used to dress up in the flags
of rival baronies and conquer one another in cold rooms of
   stone.
Out on the dance floor we were all doing the Struggle
while your sister practiced the Daphne all alone in her
   room.
We borrowed the jargon of farriers for our slang.
These days language seems transparent, a badly broken
   code.

The 1790s will never come again. Childhood was big.
People would take walks to the very tops of hills
and write down what they saw in their journals without
   speaking.
Our collars were high and our hats were extremely soft.

We would surprise each other with alphabets made of
    twigs.
It was a wonderful time to be alive, or even dead.

I am very fond of the period between 1815 and 1821.
Europe trembled while we sat still for our portraits.
And I would love to return to 1901 if only for a moment,
time enough to wind up a music box and do a few dance
    steps,
or shoot me back to 1922 or 1941, or at least let me
recapture the serenity of last month when we picked
berries and glided through afternoons in a canoe.

Even this morning would be an improvement over the
    present.
I was in the garden then, surrounded by the hum of bees
and the Latin names of flowers, watching the early light
flash off the slanted windows of the greenhouse
and silver the limbs on the rows of dark hemlocks.

As usual, I was thinking about the moments of the past,
letting my memory rush over them like water
rushing over the stones on the bottom of a stream.
I was even thinking a little about the future, that place
where people are doing a dance we cannot imagine,
a dance whose name we can only guess.

Grateful acknowledgment is made to the editors of the following magazines in which many of these poems, some in earlier versions, have appeared: *ACM, Black Warrior Review, Boulevard, Field, The Florida Review, Free Lunch, The Georgia Review, The Jacaranda Review, The Kansas Quarterly, Oxford Magazine, The Paris Review, Pearl, Slow Dancer, The Wooster Review, Wordsmith, The Wormwood Review.*

"The Afterlife," "American Sonnet," "The Death of Allegory," "First Reader," "Forgetfulness," "The History of Weather," "Mappamundi," and "Student of Clouds" first appeared in *Poetry.*

The author gratefully acknowledges the National Endowment for the Arts and the PSC-CUNY Research Award Program of the City University of New York for their generous support.

PHOTO: JOANNE CARNEY

Billy Collins is the author of five books of poetry, including *Picnic, Lightning, The Art of Drowning*—a finalist for the 1996 Lenore Marshall Prize, and *The Apple That Astonished Paris*. Collins's poetry has appeared in anthologies, textbooks, and a variety of periodicals, including *Poetry, American Poetry Review, American Scholar, Harper's, Paris Review,* and *The New Yorker*. His work has been featured in the Pushcart Prize anthology and *The Best American Poetry* for 1992, 1993, and 1997. He has received fellowships from the New York Foundation for the Arts, the National Endowment for the Arts, and the Guggenheim Foundation. He has also won the Bess Hokin Prize, the Frederick Bock Prize, the Oscar Blumenthal Prize, and the Levinson Prize— all awarded by *Poetry* magazine. In 1992, he was chosen by the New York Public Library to serve as a "Literary Lion." He has given readings at numerous colleges and other institutions. For several years he has conducted summer poetry workshops in Ireland at University College Galway. He is professor of English at Lehman College, CUNY.